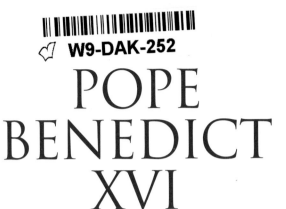
# POPE BENEDICT XVI

## THE WORD OF GOD
### IN CONVERSATION WITH GOD

*Spiritual Thoughts Series*

*Preface by Lucio Coco*
*Introduction by Archbishop Nikola Eterović*

United States Conference of Catholic Bishops
Washington, D.C.

OTHER TITLES IN THE SPIRITUAL THOUGHTS SERIES

Pope Benedict XVI, *Spiritual Thoughts in the First Year of His Papacy*

Pope Benedict XVI, *St. Paul*

Pope Benedict XVI, *Mary*

Pope Benedict XVI, *The Saints*

Photo credit: *L'Osservatore Romano*.

First printing, January 2009

ISBN: 978-1-60137-065-5

# CONTENTS

# PREFACE

*Choosing God means choosing according to his Word,*
*living according to the Word.*

—POPE BENEDICT XVI

his anthology of Pope Benedict XVI's thoughts on the theme of the Word of God—which resembles "The Word of God in the Life and Mission of the Church," the subject established by the Holy Father for the Twelfth Ordinary General Assembly of the Synod of Bishops (which took place October 5-26, 2008, at the Vatican)—provides evidence of the constant attention the Holy Father gives to Sacred Scripture and of its importance, which he recognizes, in the life of the Christian.

Together with Cyprian, Jerome, Augustine, and the other Fathers of the Church whom he presented and discussed in his weekly audiences, Pope Benedict reminds us that "to read Scripture is to converse with God" (Audience, November 14, 2007). And this appears all the more necessary today, at a time in which secularism, materialism, and relativism seem to want to eliminate any room for God and completely erase his voice through the background noise and din created by these postmodern ideologies. Pope Benedict never tires of reminding us that only where there is a true and profound meditation of the Word can we experience "this visibility, this tangibility of God in the world" (Speech, February 7, 2008) and perceive his loving presence, capable of "dispel[ling] the darkness of fear and light[ing] up the path even when times are most difficult" (Message, February 22, 2006).

But Pope Benedict is interested in stressing another moment as well: the conversation with God that we engage in when we meditate on Scripture. Recognizing the action of the Holy Spirit that opens the hearts of believers to the comprehension and understanding of what is contained in it, and following the teaching of Origen, the Holy Father urges us toward a "spiritual" reading of Scripture through which we are able to grasp its profound unity and to perceive that it is Christ who speaks to us throughout its entire development (cf. Audience, April 25, 2007). In this way, the literal meaning of the Sacred Scriptures is continually transcended in light of Christ. And it is in this light, Pope Benedict tells us, that the experience of the disciples on the road to Emmaus can be repeated—of the Lord who walks together with us, who explains the Scriptures to us, and who makes us understand that everything speaks of him (cf. Audience, March 26, 2008).

Citing St. Jerome, Pope Benedict repeats to the people of this new millennium that "ignorance of Scripture is ignorance of Christ." Therefore, like those disciples who were lost and disoriented because of all that had occurred during those days in Jerusalem (cf. Lk 24:14), we too can enter into conversation with Christ today, listening to his Word and—by becoming familiar with the Bible—reading it and using it as a compass to help us find the right reference points for searching our souls and tending toward the perfection of a life continually reflected in God and in his Incarnate Word, Jesus.

Lucio Coco

# INTRODUCTION

*There is an urgent need for the emergence of a new generation of apostles anchored firmly in the Word of Christ, capable of responding to the challenges of our time and prepared to spread the Gospel far and wide.*

—POPE BENEDICT XVI

he Word of God is one of the themes that the Holy Father, Pope Benedict XVI, makes the foundation of his instructions and exhortations that he directs to his various and numerous listeners, whether religious or faithful lay persons. He invites us to become receptive listeners to the Word that God continues to speak to us, and to live in it so as to make it present in our daily lives on the personal, family, and social levels. In this sense, Pope Benedict XVI found an additional opportunity for reflection and in-depth study in the Twelfth Ordinary General Assembly of the Synod of Bishops. The theme of the Synod was "The Word of God in the Life and Mission of the Church," to "help every Christian and every ecclesial and civil community to rediscover the importance of God's Word in their life" (Speech, January 25, 2007).

The richness of the expression "Word of God" is well emphasized in the thoughts of the Holy Father collected in this anthology. In the beginning it is the creative Word: "this Word that created all things, that created this intelligent design which is the cosmos" (Audience, November 9, 2005), the Word that reveals the Wisdom of God and the loving design that inspires him and makes the world and creation "next to Sacred Scripture . . . [as] a Bible of God" (Audience, November 28, 2007). After the Original Sin of our ancestors, man's vision became darkened, making it difficult to know God through the awareness and perception of his "*liber naturae*" [free nature]. In his immense goodness, God did not abandon man. From the beginning he revealed himself "by deeds and words"[1] to our ancestors and the patriarchs, and he spoke "many times and in various ways through the prophets" (DV, no. 4; cf. Heb 1:1). But his Revelation became complete and definitive in Christ (cf. Heb 1:2). In him, the divine Word "is no longer solely a commandment but also a gift of love, incarnate in Christ" (Speech, February 1, 2008). In him it finds its resting place in the world: he "comes to dwell in the world, many aspects of which make it a desolate valley; he shows full solidarity with human beings and brings them the glad tidings of eternal life" (Homily, November 4, 2006). Jesus, God and man, is the heart of the Word of God (cf. *Lineamenta*,[2] no. 8). Those who know God in Christ (cf. Jn 14:9) know the truth about man and the reason for his existence: "where we come from, what life is and what we are called for" (Speech, February 1, 2008). The path

---

1    Second Vatican Council, *Dogmatic Constitution on Divine Revelation* (*Dei Verbum*) (DV), no. 2, in *Vatican Council II: Volume 1: The Conciliar and Post Conciliar Documents*, ed. Austin Flannery (Northport, NY: Costello Publishing, 1996).

2    The full text of this unique resource from the 2008 Synod of Bishops can be found on the Vatican Web site at *www.vatican.va/roman_curia/synod/documents/rc_synod_doc_20070427_lineamenta-xii-assembly_en.html*.

that God shows us in his Word made flesh inscribes itself in the very essence of man. "Following the Word of God, going with Christ," the Holy Father says, "means fulfilling oneself; losing it is equivalent to losing oneself" (Homily, May 29, 2005).

In the Sacred Scriptures—where the words pronounced by God in ancient times through the prophets and especially through his only Son Jesus Christ (cf. *Lineamenta*, no. 9e) are set by divine inspiration—people of all times find the instrument that helps them to dwell in conversation with God the Father, Son, and Holy Spirit. Pope Benedict stresses the concrete nature of this encounter when he reminds us that the Good News is "not just a word, but a person" (Homily, December 1, 2006), highlighting the ontological weight of the Word of the Gospel, "which is none other than the reflection of Christ, true man and true God" (Angelus, January 1, 2008). He reveals himself in the grace of the Spirit, the face of the Father (cf. Jn 14:9). The Church, the deposit and custodian of this truth, knows very well in fact that "Christ lives in the Sacred Scriptures" (Speech, September 16, 2005). The Church has always venerated the Sacred Scriptures with the same loyalty and reverence reserved for the Body of Christ itself (cf. DV, no. 21). The Church and the Word of God, the Holy Father says, are intimately connected and inseparable: "the Church lives on the Word of God and the Word of God echoes through the Church" (Speech, September 16, 2005). By the grace of the Holy Spirit, the Word of God is fulfilled through the Church in fidelity to Revelation and in the creativity required by the people and the times.

The opening of the dogmatic constitution *Dei Verbum* points out two characteristic aspects of the Church: she is a community that, like Mary (cf. nos. 27-33 of this anthology), listens to the Word of God "with reverence" and proclaims it "with faith" (DV, no. 1). Pope Benedict emphasizes that there is a close connection between listening and announcing: "only those who first listen to the Word can become preachers of it" (Speech, September 16, 2005). At the root of the mission of the Word lies first of all this: that we are sent neither to announce ourselves or personal opinions, nor to "teach [our] own wisdom but the wisdom of God, which often appears to be foolishness in the eyes of the world (cf. 1 Cor 1:23)" (Speech, September 16, 2005). Amid the loquaciousness of our time, the inflation of often useless and empty words, this is the mission of those who believe: "to make the essential words heard . . . making present the Word, the Word who comes from God, the Word who is God" (Homily, October 6, 2006). The experience of the Apostle Paul, whose bimillenary is being celebrated in these very months, is surely the one that best describes this dynamic of listening and announcing. It is a question of continually enriching our faith experience through listening to the Word of God and proclaiming it by the witness of our lives and in the preaching of the Gospel of Jesus Christ: "we are not charged to utter many words, but to echo and bear the message of a single 'Word,' the Word of God made flesh for our salvation" (Speech, May 13, 2005). The Holy Father teaches that it is this univocality—the unique and single voice of the Lord—that should speak in the transmission of his Word to the world;

no human sound seeking to bend it toward a particular or personal point of view should contaminate it, risking a distortion of the essence itself of the Truth.

The Word, "proclaimed and listened to, seeks to become the Word celebrated in the Liturgy and the Church's sacramental life" (*Lineamenta*, no. 20). Liturgical celebrations fully express the Church's bond with the Word that nurtures and vivifies her. Pope Benedict points out that God speaks through the Liturgy in the life of the Church: "the Liturgy is the privileged place where every one of us can enter into the 'we' of the [children] of God, in conversation with God" (Speech, February 17, 2007). Celebrating the Word and making the Body of Christ present in the Sacrament, "we actualize the Word in our lives and make it present among us" (Audience, November 7, 2007). The Holy Father says that only insofar as Christian communities are eucharistic—only insofar as they nourish themselves at the double table of the Word and the Body of the Lord—can they "can transmit Christ to humanity, and not only ideas or values which are also noble and important" (Angelus, October 2, 2005). In this context of the centrality of the Word of God, Pope Benedict XVI identifies important elements that justify and motivate the other major tasks of the ecclesial community, such as evangelization and ecumenism. In the first case, it is the Lord's Revelation that provides inspiration and finality to the missionary action of the Church. In the second case, ecumenical dialogue is inspired by precisely the awareness that it "cannot base itself on words of human wisdom (cf. 1 Cor 2:13) or on neat, expedient strategies, but must be animated solely by constant reference to the original Word that God consigned to his Church so that it be read, interpreted and lived in communion with her" (Speech [1], January 21, 2008).

The Word of God, which through the power of the Holy Spirit "permeates and animates every aspect of the Church's life" (*Lineamenta*, no. 19), ensures that Sacred Scripture does not remain "locked away in writing" (*Lineamenta*, no. 9f) and that in every age it acquires the meaning of the present and living Word. It is evident, the Holy Father explains, that only where Christ remains present with us, in the body of his Church—"only where the 'Presence' is" (Homily, April 13, 2006)—can the Bible acquire meaning for us, become eloquent, and truly speak to us and teach us in our here and now. Otherwise, it falls into disarray and splinters "into heterogeneous writings and would thus . . . become a book of the past" (Homily, April 13, 2006). Instead, the Lord always remains present with us in the Church. His Word does not resonate in her like something from the past. He "speaks in the present, he speaks to us today, he enlightens us, he shows us the way through life" (Audience, March 29, 2006), giving us the awareness that we "can be friends of Jesus only in communion with the whole of Christ, with the Head and with the Body; in the vigorous vine of the Church to which the Lord gives life" (Homily, April 13, 2006).

Pope Benedict strongly insists on this approach to the Word of God, which he calls "communal," and advises that conversation with the Lord cannot be merely individual but must occur "in the great communion of the Church where Christ is ever present" (Speech, May 18, 2008).

In this way, he reminds everyone that the fundamental criterion for the interpretation of the Scriptures is harmony with the Church's Magisterium. Under the inspiration of the Holy Spirit, the Bible was written "by" and "for" the People of God, and therefore "only in this communion with the People of God do we truly enter into the 'we,' into the nucleus of the truth that God himself wants to tell us" (Audience, November 14, 2007). An authentic interpretation of the Bible must always be "in harmonious accord with the Catholic Church" (Audience, November 14, 2007); and when the Sacred Scriptures are separated from the living voice of the Church, they risk splintering and "fall[ing] prey to disputes among experts" (Homily, May 7, 2005). The Holy Father admits that the work of specialists is certainly important and valuable "in understanding the living process in which the Scriptures developed, hence, also in grasping their historical richness" (Homily, May 7, 2005). However, he also states the limitations of the historical-critical method, which by itself does not always sufficiently aid us in grasping the spirit and life of the Word of God. The interpretation of the Bible "is always also requested and called into question over and above the scientific perspective" (Speech, March 21, 2007). Pope Benedict explains that humanity needs to examine itself, to ask itself questions that transcend every form of specialization, questions concerning the essential; and when these questions are no longer asked "we no longer receive answers, either" (Speech, March 21, 2007).

Reading the Bible in personal conversation with the Lord, reading under the guidance of great teachers who have come into contact with the spirit of the Scriptures, and reading in the great company of the Church—in the interaction of these three dimensions, Pope Benedict acknowledges the correct method that believers can use in order to draw closer to the Word of God (cf. Speech, April 6, 2006). The practice of the *lectio divina* best synthesizes this experience. It constitutes a true spiritual itinerary, whose phases—reading (*lectio*), meditation (*meditatio*), prayer (*oratio*), and contemplation (*contemplatio*)—mark a path on which we learn to "encounter Jesus present, who speaks to us. We must reason and reflect, before him and with him, on his words and actions" (Homily, April 13, 2006). Nonetheless, the reading, study of, and meditation on the Word must be transformed into a life of coherent adherence to Christ. Word and witness go hand in hand. The Word, says Pope Benedict, "calls forth and gives form to the witness; the witness derives its authenticity from total fidelity to the Word" (Speech, November 7, 2005). As he pointed out in his encyclical *On Christian Hope* (*Spe Salvi*), Christianity is not a communication of content or simply of "knowledge" to others; the Christian message is not only "informative," but also "operative." The Holy Father explains what this means: "the Gospel is not merely a communication of things that can be known—it is one that makes things happen and is life-changing" (no. 2). In a society that shows its disorientation in various ways today more than ever—a disorientation characterized, for example, by the crisis of values—Pope Benedict tells us that the Word of God is always "a Word that builds" (Homily, December 10, 2006). It remains creative in its essence. It transcends the letter in order to remain engraved in individual lives and in the collective history of humanity: creating meaning and bringing Truth, who is God, the one who alone has the words of eternal life (cf. Jn 6:68), and Christ the Incarnate Word (cf. Jn 14:6), "the Father's one, perfect, and unsurpassable Word" (*Catechism of the Catholic Church*, no. 65).

Archbishop Nikola Eterovic
*Secretary General of the Synod of Bishops*

# THE WORD OF GOD

*The Word of God . . . indicates the path of life to man
and reveals the secrets of holiness to him.*

—POPE BENEDICT XVI, AUDIENCE, NOVEMBER 14, 2007

### 1. *Hearing with reverence*

The Dogmatic Constitution *Dei Verbum* . . . begins with a
deeply meaningful [phrase]: "*Dei Verbum religiose audiens
. . .*" ["Hearing the Word of God with reverence . . ."]. . . .
This is a point that every Christian must understand and
apply to himself or herself: only those who first listen to
the Word can become preachers of it. Indeed, they must
not teach their own wisdom but the wisdom of God, which
often appears to be foolishness in the eyes of the world
(cf. 1 Cor 1:23).

*Address on the fortieth anniversary of* Dei Verbum
*September 16, 2005*

# I. Divine Revelation

*It pleased God, in his goodness and wisdom, to reveal himself and to make known the mystery of his will.*

—Second Vatican Council, *Dei Verbum*, no. 2

## 1. The Creative Word

*2. "In the beginning was the Word" (Jn 1:1)*

The Lord through Sacred Scripture reawakens our reason which has fallen asleep and tells us: in the beginning was the creative Word. In the beginning the creative Word—this Word that created all things, that created this intelligent design which is the cosmos—is also love. Therefore, let us allow this Word of God to awaken us; let us pray that it will additionally illumine our minds so that we can perceive the message of creation—also written in our hearts—that the beginning of all things is creative wisdom, and this wisdom is love, it is goodness.

*General Audience*
*November 9, 2005*

## 3. *Free nature*

Nothing in creation is isolated and the world, next to Sacred Scripture, is a Bible of God.

*General Audience*
*November 28, 2007*

# 2. Jesus, the Heart of the Word of God

### 4. *The Word Incarnate*

The divine Word, incarnate in Jesus, comes to dwell in the world, many aspects of which make it a desolate valley; he shows full solidarity with human beings and brings them the glad tidings of eternal life.

*Homily at Mass for the souls of cardinals and bishops*
*November 4, 2006*

### 5. *The Good News*

This Good News is not just a word, but a person, Christ himself, risen and alive!

*Homily at Mass in Istanbul, Turkey*
*December 1, 2006*

## 6. *Christ the Word*

The path God points out to us through his Word goes in the direction inscribed in man's very existence. The Word of God and reason go together. For the human being, following the Word of God, going with Christ means fulfilling oneself; losing it is equivalent to losing oneself.

> *Homily at Mass in Marisabella, Italy*
> *May 29, 2005*

## 7. *Jesus Christ in Sacred Scripture*

Help people to discover the true star which points out the way to us: Jesus Christ! Let us seek to know him better and better, so as to be able to guide others to him with conviction. This is why love for Sacred Scripture is so important.

> *Homily at Mass for the Twentieth World Youth Day*
> *August 21, 2005*

## 8. *Encounter*

We meet Jesus in listening to the Sacred Scriptures.

> *Homily at Mass in Santa Maria del Rosario Parish, Rome*
> *December 16, 2007*

## 9. *"Ignorance of Scripture is ignorance of Christ"* *(St. Jerome)*

It is also important for us not to reduce ourselves merely to the superficiality of the many who have heard something about him—that he was an important figure, etc.—but to enter into a personal relationship to know him truly. And this demands knowledge of Scripture, especially of the Gospels where the Lord speaks to us. These words are not always easy, but in entering into them, entering into dialogue, knocking at the door of words, saying to the Lord, "Let me in," we truly find words of eternal life, living words for today, as timely as they were then and as they will be in the future.

*Meeting with young people of Genoa, Italy*
*May 18, 2005*

## 10. *In dialogue with Jesus*

Also today we can enter into dialogue with Jesus, listening to his Word.

*Regina Caeli*
*April 6, 2008*

## 11. *Listening to Christ*

[We need] to listen to [Christ] in his Word, contained in Sacred Scripture. To listen to him in the events of our lives, seeking to decipher in them the messages of Providence. Finally, to listen to him in our brothers and sisters, especially in the lowly and the poor, to whom Jesus himself demands our concrete love. To listen to Christ and obey his voice: this is the principal way, the only way, that leads to the fullness of joy and of love.

*Angelus*
*March 12, 2006*

## 12. *The gift of the Word*

Jesus, coming from the Father, visited people's homes on our earth and found a humanity that was sick, sick with fever, the fever of ideologies, idolatry, forgetfulness of God. The Lord gives us his hand, lifts us up and heals us. And he does so in all ages; he takes us by the hand with his Word, thereby dispelling the fog of ideologies and forms of idolatry. . . . The Lord comes to meet us, he takes us by the hand, raises us and heals us ever anew with the gift of his words, the gift of himself.

*Homily at Mass in St. Anne's Parish, Vatican City*
*February 5, 2006*

### 13. *The living Word of Christ*

The Word of God is no longer solely a commandment but also a gift of love, incarnate in Christ. We can really say: thank you, Lord, for giving us this gift of knowing you; those who know you in Christ therefore know the living word and know in the obscurity, in the many enigmas of this world, in the many unsolvable problems, the way to go; we know where we come from, what life is and what we are called for.

*Meeting with seminarians at the Roman Major Seminary*
*February 1, 2008*

### 14. *The "short" Word*

The Fathers of the Church, in their Greek translation of the Old Testament, found a passage from the prophet Isaiah that Paul also quotes in order to show how God's new ways had already been foretold in the Old Testament. There we read: "God made his Word short, he abbreviated it" (Is 10:23; Rom 9:28). . . . The Word which God speaks to us in Sacred Scripture had become long in the course of the centuries. It became long and complex, not just for the simple and unlettered, but even more so for those versed in Sacred Scripture, for the experts who evidently became entangled in details and in particular problems, almost to the extent of losing an overall perspective. Jesus "abbreviated" the Word—he showed us once more its deeper simplicity and unity. Everything taught by the Law and the Prophets is summed up—he says—in the command: "You shall love the Lord your God with all your heart, and with all your soul, and with all your mind. . . . You shall love your neighbor as yourself" (Mt 22:37-40). This is everything—the whole faith is contained in this one act of love which embraces God and humanity.

*Homily at Midnight Mass, Christmas Day*
*December 25, 2006*

### 15. *Christ explains the Scriptures*

Throughout the liturgical year, particularly in Holy Week and Easter Week, the Lord walks beside us and explains the Scriptures to us, makes us understand this mystery: everything speaks of him. And this should also make our hearts burn within us, so that our eyes too may be opened. The Lord is with us, he shows us the true path.

*General Audience*
*March 26, 2008*

## 16. *Following the Lamb*

The Lamb, Jesus, leads men and women to the sources of life. Among these sources are the Sacred Scriptures, in which God speaks to us and tells us the how to live in the right way. But there is more to these sources: in truth the authentic source is Jesus himself, in whom God gives us his very self.

*Homily at Vespers in the Cathedral of Munich*
*September 10, 2006*

# II. LISTENING TO THE WORD OF GOD

*Our relationship with God takes place more by listening than by seeing . . . thanks to the interior light that is kindled in us by the Word of God.*

—POPE BENEDICT XVI, ANGELUS, MARCH 12, 2006

17. *Listening*

Living the Word of God to the full demands attentive listening and a generous and mature heart.

*Meeting with members of Sacra Famiglia di Nazareth and Comunità Domenico Tardini associations November 11, 2006*

## 18. *With an understanding heart*

The secret of acquiring *"an understanding heart"* [1 Kgs 3:9] is to train your heart to *listen*. This is obtained by persistently meditating on the word of God and by remaining firmly rooted in it through the commitment to persevere in getting to know it better.

*Message for the Twenty-First World Youth Day*
*February 22, 2006*

## 19. *Discernment*

How can we distinguish God's voice from among the thousands of voices we hear each day in our world[?] I would say: God speaks with us in many different ways. He speaks through others, through friends, parents, pastors, priests. . . . He speaks by means of the events in our life, in which we are able to discern God's touch; he speaks also through nature, creation, and he speaks, naturally and above all, through his Word, in Sacred Scripture, read in the communion of the Church and read personally in conversation with God.

*Visit to the Roman Major Seminary*
*February 17, 2007*

## 20. *In conversation with God*

It is important to read Sacred Scripture in a very personal way, and really, as St. Paul says, not as a human word or a document from the past as we read Homer or Virgil, but as God's Word which is ever timely and speaks to me. It is important to learn to understand in a historical text, a text from the past, the living Word of God, that is, to enter into prayer and thus read Sacred Scripture as a conversation with God.

*Visit to the Roman Major Seminary*
*February 17, 2007*


## 21. *Dialogue*

To dialogue with God, with his Word, is in a certain sense a presence of Heaven, a presence of God. To draw near to the biblical texts, above all the New Testament, is essential for the believer, because "ignorance of the Scriptures is ignorance of Christ" (St. Jerome, *Commentary on Isaiah*, Prologue, PL 24:17).

*General Audience*
*November 14, 2007*

## 22. *Choosing God*

Choosing God means choosing according to his words, living according to the Word.

*Meeting with priests and clergy of the Diocese of Rome*
*February 7, 2008*


## 23. *Faith in the Word*

Only if each one of the faithful allows his or her personal and community life to be joined to the Word of Christ, who asks for a personal and adult response of faith through authentic and lasting conversion with a view to social fruitfulness and brotherhood among all, can the Gospel profoundly illumine their consciences and transform cultures from within.

*Address to the bishops of Congo*
*during their* ad limina *visit*
*January 27, 2006*

## 24. *Living the Word*

The Christian's life is a life of faith, founded on the Word of God and nourished by it. In the trials of life and in every temptation, the secret of victory lies in listening to the Word of truth and rejecting with determination falsehood and evil. This is the true and central program of [the Christian]: to listen to the word of truth, to live, speak and do what is true, to refuse falsehood that poisons humanity and is the vehicle of all evils.

*General Audience*
*March 1, 2006*

## 25. *Listening and obeying*

The author of the Letter to the Hebrews wrote: "Indeed, the word of God is living and active, sharper than any two-edged sword, piercing until it divides soul from spirit, joints from marrow; it is able to judge the thoughts and intentions of the heart" (4:12). It is necessary to take seriously the injunction to consider the word of God to be an indispensable "weapon" in the spiritual struggle. This will be effective and show results if we learn to *listen* to it and then to *obey* it.

*Message for the Twenty-First World Youth Day*
*February 22, 2006*

## 26. *Space for listening*

In an age when the influence of secularization is always more powerful and, on the other hand, one senses a diffused need to encounter God, may the possibility to offer spaces for intense listening to his Word in silence and prayer always be available.

*Address at the assembly of the Italian*
*Federation of Spiritual Exercises*
*February 9, 2008*

# III. Mary, Model of Welcoming the Word

*Listen to Christ, like Mary.*

—Pope Benedict XVI

27. *Awe of the Word*

The Virgin receives the heavenly Messenger while she is intent on meditating upon the Sacred Scriptures, usually shown by a book that Mary holds in her hand, on her lap or on a lectern. This is also the image of the Church which the Council itself offered in the Constitution *Dei Verbum*: "Hearing the Word of God with reverence . . ." (no. 1). Let us pray that like Mary, the Church will be a humble handmaid of the divine Word and will always proclaim it with firm trust, so that "the whole world . . . through hearing it may believe, through belief . . . may hope, through hope . . . may come to love" (*Dei Verbum*, no. 1).

*Angelus*
*November 6, 2005*

28. *An icon of the Annunciation*

[In this depiction of the Annunciation of Mary,] the Archangel Gabriel holds a scroll in his hand, which I believe is the symbol of Scripture, of the Word of God. And Mary is kneeling within the scroll; that is, she lives her whole life in the Word of God. It is as though she were steeped in the Word. Thus, all her thoughts, her will and her actions are imbued with and formed by the Word. Since she herself dwells in the Word, she can also become the new "Dwelling Place" of the Word in the world.

*Address at the close of the papal spiritual exercises*
*March 11, 2006*

29. *Living on the Word of God*

Mary's poem—the *Magnificat*—is quite original; yet at the same time, it is a "fabric" woven throughout of "threads" from the Old Testament, of words of God. Thus, we see that Mary was, so to speak, "at home" with God's word, she lived on God's word, she was penetrated by God's word. To the extent that she spoke with God's words, she thought with God's words, her thoughts were God's thoughts, her words, God's words. She was penetrated by divine light and this is why she was so resplendent, so good, so radiant with love and goodness. Mary lived on the Word of God, she was imbued with the Word of God. And the fact that she was immersed in the Word of God and was totally familiar with the Word also endowed her later with the inner enlightenment of wisdom. Whoever thinks with God thinks well, and whoever speaks to God speaks well.

*Homily at Mass for the Feast of the Assumption*
*August 15, 2005*

## 30. *Imitating Mary*

Mary speaks with us, speaks to us, invites us to know the Word of God, to love the Word of God, to live with the Word of God, to think with the Word of God. And we can do so in many different ways: by reading Sacred Scripture, by participating especially in the Liturgy, in which Holy Church throughout the year opens the entire book of Sacred Scripture to us. She opens it to our lives and makes it present in our lives.

*Homily at Mass for the Feast of the Assumption*
*August 15, 2005*

## 31. *Nourishment of the Word and eucharistic Bread*

Mary helps us to meet the Lord above all in the celebration of the Eucharist, when, in the Word and in the consecrated Bread, he becomes our daily spiritual nourishment.

*Meeting with seminarians in Cologne*
*August 19, 2005*

## 32. *Mary and the Church*

The Gospel adds that Mary "treasured all these things and reflected on them in her heart" (Lk 2:19). Like Mary, the Church also treasures and reflects upon the Word of God, comparing it to the various changing situations she encounters on her way.

*Angelus*
*January 1, 2006*

## 33. *Prayer to Mary*

Holy Mary, Mother of God, pray for us so that we may live the Gospel. Help us not to hide the light of the Gospel under the bushel of our meager faith. Help us by virtue of the Gospel to be the light of the world, so that men and women may see goodness and glorify the Father who is in Heaven (cf. Mt 5:14ff.). Amen!

*Homily at Our Lady Star of Evangelization Parish, Rome*
*December 10, 2006*

# IV. THE WORD OF GOD IN THE LIFE OF THE CHURCH

*The Scriptures are then in the heart and hands of the Church as the "Letter sent by God to humankind" (St. Gregory the Great).*

—LINEAMENTA OF THE 2008 SYNOD OF BISHOPS

## 1. The Presence of the Word of God in the Church

34. *The Word of God, nourishment of the Church*

The Church does not make herself or live of herself, but from the creative Word that comes from the mouth of God.

*Homily at Vespers for the Feast of the Conversion of St. Paul January 25, 2007*

## 35. The Word and the People of God

Believing is in itself a Catholic act. It is participation in this great certainty, which is present in the Church as a living subject. Only in this way can we also understand Sacred Scripture in the diversity of an interpretation that develops for thousands of years. It is a Scripture because it is an element, an expression of the unique subject—the People of God—which on its pilgrimage is always the same subject. Of course, it is a subject that does not speak of itself, but is created by God—the classical expression is "inspired"—a subject that receives, then translates and communicates this word. This synergy is very important.

*Meeting with members of the Roman clergy*
*March 2, 2006*

## 36. Inspiration by the Holy Spirit

Sacred Scripture is a journey with a direction. Those who know the destination can also take all those steps once again now, and can thus acquire a deeper knowledge of the Mystery of Christ. In understanding this, we have also understood the ecclesiality of Sacred Scripture, for these journeys, these steps on the journey, are the steps of a people. It is the People of God who are moving onwards. The true owner of the Word is always the People of God, guided by the Holy Spirit, and inspiration is a complex process: the Holy Spirit leads the people on, the people receive it.

*Lenten meeting with the clergy of Rome*
*February 22, 2007*

### 37. Synergy of the Word and People of God

Sacred Scripture has two subjects. First and foremost, the divine subject: it is God who is speaking. However, God wanted to involve man in his Word. Whereas Muslims are convinced that the Koran was verbally inspired by God, we believe that for Sacred Scripture it is "synergy"—as the theologians say—that is characteristic, the collaboration of God with man. God involves his People with his Word, hence, the second subject—the first subject, as I said, is God—is human. There are individual writers, but there is the continuity of a permanent subject—the People of God that journeys on with the Word of God and is in conversation with God. By listening to God, one learns to listen to the Word of God and then also to interpret it. Thus, the Word of God becomes present, because individual persons die but the vital subject, the People of God, is always alive and is identical in the course of the millenniums: it is always the same living subject in which the Word lives.

*Meeting with youth in Rome before the*
*Twenty-First World Youth Day*
*April 6, 2006*

## 38. *The Church and the Word*

The Church and the Word of God are inseparably linked. The Church lives on the Word of God and the Word of God echoes through the Church, in her teaching and throughout her life (cf. *Dei Verbum*, no. 8). The Apostle Peter, therefore, reminds us that no prophecy contained in Scripture can be subjected to a personal interpretation. "Prophecy has never been put forward by man's willing it. It is rather that men impelled by the Holy Spirit have spoken under God's influence" (2 Pt 1:20).

*Address on the fortieth anniversary of* Dei Verbum
*September 16, 2005*

## 39. *In communion with the Church*

Day after day, we must deepen our communion with the Holy Church and thus, with the Word of God. They are not two opposite things, so that I can say: I am pro-Church or I am pro-God's Word. Only when we are united in the Church, do we belong to the Church, do we become members of the Church, do we live by the Word of God which is the life-giving force of the Church. And those who live by the Word of God can only live it because it is alive and vital in the living Church.

*Meeting with members of the Roman clergy*
*March 2, 2006*

## 40. *The institution of the Church*

In the Church, the institution is not merely an external structure while the Gospel is purely spiritual. In fact, the Gospel and the Institution are inseparable because the Gospel has a body, the Lord has a body in this time of ours. Consequently, issues that seem at first sight merely institutional are actually theological and central, because it is a matter of the realization and concretization of the Gospel in our time.

*Address to the bishops of Switzerland*
*November 9, 2006*


## 41. *Scripture and the Church*

The Church knows well that Christ lives in the Sacred Scriptures. For this very reason—as the Constitution stresses—she has always venerated the divine Scriptures in the same way as she venerates the Body of the Lord (cf. *Dei Verbum*, no. 21). In view of this, St. Jerome, cited by the conciliar Document, said that ignorance of the Scriptures is ignorance of Christ (cf. *Dei Verbum*, no. 25).

*Address on the fortieth anniversary of* Dei Verbum
*September 16, 2005*

## 42. *Communal reading of Sacred Scripture*

In addition to . . . personal reading, reading [Scripture] in the community is very important because the living subject of Sacred Scripture is the People of God, it is the Church. This Scripture was not simply restricted to great writers—even if the Lord always needs the person and his personal response—but it developed with people who were traveling together on the journey of the People of God and thus, their words are expressions of this journey, of this reciprocity of God's call and the human response.

*Visit to the Roman Major Seminary*
*February 17, 2007*

# 2. Scripture and Tradition

43. *The Bible in the Church*

We can be friends of Jesus only in communion with the whole of Christ, with the Head and with the Body; in the vigorous vine of the Church to which the Lord gives life. Sacred Scripture is a living and actual Word, thanks to the Lord, only in [the Church]. Without the living subject of the Church that embraces the ages, more often than not the Bible would have splintered into heterogeneous writings and would thus have become a book of the past. It is eloquent in the present only where the "Presence" is—where Christ remains for ever contemporary with us: in the Body of his Church.

*Homily at Holy Thursday Chrism Mass*
*April 13, 2006*

## 44. *Tradition and Scripture*

The Apostles and their successors, the Bishops, are depositories of the message that Christ entrusted to his Church so that it might be passed on in its integrity to all generations. Sacred Scripture of the Old and New Testaments and sacred Tradition contain this message, whose understanding develops in the Church with the help of the Holy Spirit. This same Tradition makes known the integral canon of the sacred Books. It makes them directly understandable and operative so that God, who has spoken to the Patriarchs and Prophets, does not cease to speak to the Church and through her, to the world.

*Angelus*
*November 6, 2005*

## 45. *The Tradition of the Church*

Throughout the history of the Church, the Apostles preached the word of Christ, taking care to hand it on intact to their successors, who in their turn transmitted it to subsequent generations until our own day. Many preachers of the Gospel gave their lives specifically because of their faithfulness to the truth of the word of Christ. And so solicitude for the truth gave birth to the Church's Tradition. As in past centuries, so also today there are people or groups who obscure this centuries-old Tradition, seeking to falsify the Word of Christ and to remove from the Gospel those truths which in their view are too uncomfortable for modern man. They try to give the impression that everything is relative: even the truths of faith would depend on the historical situation and on human evaluation. Yet the Church cannot silence the Spirit of Truth.

*Homily at Mass in Piłsudzki Square, Warsaw*
*May 26, 2006*

## 46. *Renewal of the Church*

In the prayerful reading of Scripture and in consistent commitment to life, the Church is ever renewed and rejuvenated. The Word of God, which never ages and is never exhausted, is a privileged means to this end. Indeed, it is the Word of God, through the action of the Holy Spirit, which always guides us to the whole truth.

*General Audience*
*April 25, 2007*

## 47. *Current relevance of the Word of God*

I am convinced, in faith, that in Christ, in his word, we find the way not only to eternal happiness, but also to the building of a humane future even now, on this our land. Impelled by this conviction, the Church, led by the Spirit, has constantly looked to the Word of God so as to be able to respond to new historical challenges.

*Farewell address to Germany from the airport in Munich*
*September 14, 2006*


## 48. *Christ as contemporary of his Church*

In the Church, the Lord always remains our contemporary. Scripture is not something of the past. The Lord does not speak in the past but speaks in the present, he speaks to us today, he enlightens us, he shows us the way through life, he gives us communion and thus he prepares us and opens us to peace.

*General Audience*
*March 29, 2006*

# V. THE LITURGY OF THE WORD OF GOD

*[Christ] is present in his word since it is he himself who speaks when the holy scriptures are read in the Church.*

—SECOND VATICAN COUNCIL,
*SACROSANCTUM CONCILIUM*, NO. 7

### 49. *Present Word*

The privileged place for reading and listening to the Word of God is the liturgy, in which, celebrating the Word and making Christ's Body present in the Sacrament, we actualize the Word in our lives and make it present among us.

*General Audience*
*November 7, 2007*

## 50. *Enthroning of the Word*

Every day of the Council the Gospel was enthroned. . . .
The liturgical enthronement of the Word of God every day
during the Council was always an act of great importance:
it told us who was the true Lord of that Assembly, it told us
that the Word of God is on the throne and that we exercise
the ministry to listen to and interpret this Word in order to
offer it to others. To enthrone the Word of God, the living
Word or Christ, in the world underlies the meaning of all
we do. May it truly be he who governs our personal life
and our life in the parishes.

*Meeting with the clergy of Rome*
*February 7, 2008*


## 51. *The "we" of the Word*

[The] Word . . . becomes vital and alive in the Liturgy. I
would say, therefore, that the Liturgy is the privileged place
where every one of us can enter into the "we" of the sons
of God, in conversation with God. This is important. The
Our Father begins with the words "Our Father"; only if
I am integrated into the "we" of this "Our" can I find
the Father; only within this "we," which is the subject
of the prayer of the Our Father, do we hear the Word of
God clearly.

*Visit to the Roman Major Seminary*
*February 17, 2007*

## 52. *The altar of the Word*

The word of God must be listened to and accepted in a spirit of communion with the Church and with a clear awareness of its unity with the sacrament of the Eucharist. Indeed, the word which we proclaim and accept is the Word made flesh (cf. Jn 1:14); it is inseparably linked to Christ's person and the sacramental mode of his continued presence in our midst. Christ does not speak in the past, but in the present, even as he is present in the liturgical action. In this sacramental context of Christian revelation, knowledge and study of the word of God enable us better to appreciate, celebrate and live the Eucharist.

> *Post-Synodal Apostolic Exhortation* The Sacrament of Charity (Sacramentum Caritatis), *no. 45*
> *February 22, 2007*

## 53. *The bread of the Word*

Christian communities without the Eucharistic celebration, in which one is nourished at the double table of the Word and the Body of Christ, would lose their authentic nature: only those that are "eucharistic" can transmit Christ to humanity, and not only ideas or values which are also noble and important.

> *Angelus*
> *October 2, 2005*

## 54. The Mass

In every Mass the liturgy of the Word introduces us to our participation in the mystery of the Cross and Resurrection of Christ and hence, introduces us to the Eucharistic Meal, to union with Christ.

*Welcome to young people for the*
*Twentieth World Youth Day*
*August 18, 2005*

## 55. After the liturgy

If our Eucharistic celebration and the Liturgy of the Hours are to remain meaningful, we need to devote ourselves constantly anew to the spiritual reading of sacred Scripture; not only to be able to decipher and explain words from the distant past, but to discover the word of comfort that the Lord is now speaking to me, the Lord who challenges me by this word. Only in this way will we be capable of bringing the inspired Word to the men and women of our time as the contemporary and living Word of God.

*Homily at Vespers in the Basilica of St. Anne, Altötting*
*September 11, 2006*

# VI. THE TRANSMISSION OF THE WORD

*The duty of the mission is to bring Christ.*

—POPE BENEDICT XVI

## 1. The Mission of the Word

*56. Service*

We are not sent to proclaim ourselves or our personal opinions, but the mystery of Christ and, in him, the measure of true humanism. We are not charged to utter many words, but to echo and bear the message of a single "Word," the Word of God made flesh for our salvation. Consequently, these words of Jesus also apply to us: "My doctrine is not my own; it comes from him who sent me" (Jn 7:16).

*Address to the clergy of Rome*
*May 13, 2005*

## 57. Expressing the Word

This is [the] mission: in the loquacity of our day and of other times, in the plethora of words, to make the essential words heard. Through words, it means making present the Word, the Word who comes from God, the Word who is God.

*Homily at Mass with members of the*
*International Theological Commission*
*October 6, 2006*

## 58. Need for the Word

In this sense, I believe we [in the Church] have an important task, namely, to show that this Word which we possess is not part of the trash of history, so to speak, but it is necessary today.

*Interview before the papal visit to Bavaria*
*August 5, 2006*

## 59. *Proclaiming the Word*

We must spare no effort to ensure that the Word is listened to and known. Today, there are numerous schools of the Word and of the conversation with God in Sacred Scripture, a conversation which necessarily also becomes prayer, because the purely theoretical study of Sacred Scripture is a form of listening that is merely intellectual and would not be a real or satisfactory encounter with the Word of God. If it is true that in Scripture and in the Word of God it is the Living Lord God who speaks to us, who elicits our response and our prayers, then schools of Scripture must also be schools of prayer, of dialogue with God, of drawing intimately close to God: consequently, the whole proclamation.

*Meeting with the clergy of Belluno-Feltre and Treviso*
*July 24, 2007*

## 60. *Mission*

The Word of the Gospel . . . is still able today to guide every person to Jesus. This same Word, which is none other than the reflection of Christ, true man and true God, is authoritatively echoed by the Church for every well-disposed heart.

*Angelus*
*January 6, 2006*

# 2. In Service to the Word

### 61. *The work of bishops*

We are always in need of the work of the Bishops who, in contact with the priests and catechists, help find all the necessary instruments to facilitate this sowing of the Word.

*Address to the clergy of Aosta*
*July 25, 2005*

### 62. *The priest and the Scriptures*

Thus, on the one hand, "girded" and in "priestly attire" mean purity and honesty of life; and on the other, with the "lamp ever alight," that is, faith and knowledge of the Scriptures, we have the indispensable conditions for the exercise of the universal priesthood, which demands purity and an honest life, faith and knowledge of the Scriptures.

*General Audience*
*May 2, 2007*

## 63. *Men and women religious*

All Christians are brought together by the Word, to live of the Word and to remain under its lordship. It is therefore the special duty of men and women religious "to remind the baptized of the fundamental values of the Gospel" (*Vita Consecrata*, no. 33).

*Address for the World Day of Consecrated Life*
*February 2, 2008*

## 64. *Deacons*

Many of you [deacons] work in offices, hospitals and schools: in these contexts you are called to be servants of the Truth. By proclaiming the Gospel, you will be able to convey the Word that can illumine and give meaning to human work, to the suffering of the sick, and you will help the new generations to discover the beauty of the Christian faith. Thus you will be deacons of the liberating Truth, and you will lead the inhabitants of this city to encounter Jesus Christ.

*Address to the permanent deacons of Rome*
*February 18, 2006*

# 3. Catechesis

65. *Corresponding to the Gospel*

The successors of the Apostles, together with the Pope, are responsible for the truth of the Gospel, and all Christians are called to share in this responsibility, accepting its authoritative indications. Every Christian is bound to confront his own convictions continually with the teachings of the Gospel and of the Church's Tradition in the effort to remain faithful to the word of Christ, even when it is demanding and, humanly speaking, hard to understand. We must not yield to the temptation of relativism or of a subjectivist and selective interpretation of Sacred Scripture. Only the whole truth can open us to adherence to Christ, dead and risen for our salvation.

*Homily at Mass in Piłsudzki Square, Warsaw*
*May 26, 2006*

## 66. *Preparation of the faithful*

"Ignorance of Scripture is ignorance of Christ" (St. Jerome, *Commentary on Isaiah*, Prologue, PL 24:17). To this end, the faithful should be helped to appreciate the riches of Sacred Scripture found in the lectionary through pastoral initiatives, liturgies of the word and reading in the context of prayer (*lectio divina*). Efforts should also be made to encourage those forms of prayer confirmed by tradition, such as the Liturgy of the Hours, especially Morning Prayer, Evening Prayer and Night Prayer, and vigil celebrations. By praying the Psalms, the Scripture readings and the readings drawn from the great tradition which are included in the Divine Office, we can come to a deeper experience of the Christ-event and the economy of salvation, which in turn can enrich our understanding and participation in the celebration of the Eucharist.

> *Post-Synodal Apostolic Exhortation* The Sacrament of Charity (Sacramentum Caritatis), *no. 45*
> *February 22, 2007*

## 67. *The living water of Christ*

The people are thirsty and try to satisfy this thirst with various palliatives. But they understand well that these diversions are not the "living water" that they need. The Lord is the source of "living water." But he says in chapter 7 of John that he who believes becomes a "river" because he has drunk from Christ. And this "living water" (cf. Jn 7:38) becomes a fountain of water in us, a source for others. In this way we seek to drink it in prayer, in the celebration of Holy Mass, in reading: we seek to drink from this source so that it may become a source within us.

*Meeting with the priests of the Diocese of Albano*
*August 31, 2006*

68. *Explanation of the Scriptures*

In this regard, the question which, according to Luke's account in the Acts of the Apostles, the Deacon Philip asked the Ethiopian he met on the road from Jerusalem to Gaza, "Do you understand what you are reading?" (Acts 8:30), can be enlightening. The Ethiopian answered him: "How can I, unless someone guides me?" (8:31). Philip then spoke to him of Christ. Thus, the Ethiopian discovered the answer to his questions in the person of Christ, proclaimed in the prophet Isaiah's veiled words. It is important, therefore, that someone be beside those who are on their way and proclaim to them "the Good News of Jesus" (8:35), as Philip did. Sketched here is the "*diakonia*" [service] which Christian culture can carry out in helping those who are searching to discover the One who is concealed in the biblical passage, as well as in the events of every person's life.

*Meeting with members of Sacra Famiglia di Nazareth*
*and Comunità Domenico Tardini associations*
*November 11, 2006*

### 69. *Ambrosian catechesis*

Ambrose read the Scriptures with his mouth shut, only with his eyes (cf. St. Augustine, *Confessions*, 6, 3). Indeed, in the early Christian centuries reading was conceived of strictly for proclamation, and reading aloud also facilitated the reader's understanding. That Ambrose could scan the pages with his eyes alone suggested to the admiring Augustine a rare ability for reading and familiarity with the Scriptures. Well, in that "reading under one's breath," where the heart is committed to achieving knowledge of the Word of God . . . one can glimpse the method of Ambrosian catechesis; it is Scripture itself, intimately assimilated, which suggests the content to proclaim that will lead to the conversion of hearts.

*General Audience*
*October 24, 2007*

# 4. Evangelization

70. *The spreading of the Word*

The Book of the Acts of the Apostles, after the description of brotherhood achieved in the Christian community, points out, almost as a logical consequence, that "the Word of God continued to spread, while at the same time the number of the disciples in Jerusalem enormously increased" (Acts 6:7). The spreading of the Word is the Blessing the Lord of the harvest gives to the community that takes seriously its commitment to increase love in brotherhood.

*Address to consecrated religious, secular institutes, and societies of apostolic life of the Diocese of Rome*
*December 10, 2005*

71. *Proclamation*

I think that by looking at history's progress it is possible today to understand better that this presence of the Word of God, this proclamation which, like leaven, reaches everyone, is necessary in order that the world truly achieve its goal.

*Meeting with clergy of the Diocese of Rome*
*February 7, 2008*

## 72. *Mission*

German priests are working, even in Papua New Guinea, the Solomon Islands and regions beyond the wildest imagination, scattering the seed of the Word, identifying with people. Thus, they imbue this threatened world, invaded by so many negative things from the West, with the great power of faith and with it, all that is positive in what we are given.

*Meeting with the bishops of Germany*
*August 21, 2005*

## 73. *Serving the Gospel*

The witness of love, the soul of the mission, concerns everyone. Indeed, serving the Gospel should not be considered a solitary adventure but a commitment to be shared by every community.

*Message for the Eightieth World Mission Sunday*
*April 29, 2006*

## 74. *The communion of Christians*

To listen to the word of God together . . . letting ourselves be amazed by the newness of the Word of God that never ages and is never depleted; overcoming our deafness to those words that do not correspond with our prejudices and our opinions; to listen and also to study, in the communion of believers of all ages: all these things constitute a path to be taken in order to achieve unity in the faith as a response to listening to the Word.

*Homily at Vespers for the Feast of the*
*Conversion of St. Paul*
*January 25, 2007*

## 75. *For ecumenical dialogue*

Lastly, here are a few brief words on *ecumenism*. All the praiseworthy *initiatives on the journey to the full unity of all Christians* find common prayer and reflection on the Holy Scriptures [to be] fertile soil in which to grow and develop communion.

*Address to the bishops of Germany*
*on their* ad limina *visit*
*November 18, 2006*

## 76. *Evangelization and ecumenism*

Evangelization and ecumenism. . . . are centered on the Word of God and at the same time are justified and sustained by it. As the Church's missionary activity with its evangelizing work is inspired and aims at the merciful revelation of the Lord, ecumenical dialogue cannot base itself on words of human wisdom (cf. 1 Cor 2:13) or on neat, expedient strategies, but must be animated solely by constant reference to the original Word that God consigned to his Church so that it be read, interpreted and lived in communion with her.

*Address to the General Secretariat*
*of the Synod of Bishops*
*January 21, 2008*


## 77. *The impetus of* Dei Verbum

The conciliar Constitution *Dei Verbum* emphasized appreciation for the Word of God, which developed into a profound renewal for the life of the Ecclesial Community, especially in preaching, catechesis, theology, spirituality and ecumenical relations. Indeed, it is the Word of God which guides believers, through the action of the Holy Spirit, towards all truth (cf. Jn 16:13).

*Angelus*
*November 6, 2005*

# VII. INTERPRETING THE WORD OF GOD

*Whoever has experienced the spiritual sense of the Scriptures knows that the simplest word of Scripture and the most profound are uniquely one, both having the salvation of humankind as their purpose.*

—St. Peter Damascene

## 1. Exegesis and Magisterium

78. *Reading with the heart*

Knowledge of the Scriptures requires prayer and intimacy with Christ even more than study.

*General Audience*
*May 2, 2007*

## 79. *The multidimensionality of the Word*

[According to Origen] there is the "literal" sense, but this conceals depths that are not immediately apparent. The second dimension is the "moral" sense: what we must do in living the word; and finally, the "spiritual" sense, the unity of Scripture which throughout its development speaks of Christ. It is the Holy Spirit who enables us to understand the Christological content, hence, the unity in diversity of Scripture.

*General Audience*
*April 25, 2007*

## 80. *Theology and exegesis*

[The "irreversible turning point" of Origen] corresponds in substance to theology's foundation in the explanation of the Scriptures. Theology to him was essentially explaining, understanding Scripture; or we might also say that his theology was a perfect symbiosis between theology and exegesis. In fact, the proper hallmark of Origen's doctrine seems to lie precisely in the constant invitation to move from the letter to the spirit of the Scriptures, to progress in knowledge of God.

*General Audience*
*April 25, 2007*

## 81. *Word and exegesis*

The Word is always greater than the exegesis of the Fathers and critical exegesis because even this comprehends only a part, indeed, a minimal part. The Word is always greater, this is our immense consolation. And on the one hand it is lovely to know that one has only understood a little. It is lovely to know that there is still an inexhaustible treasure and that every new generation will rediscover new treasures and journey on with the greatness of the Word of God that is always before us, guides us and is ever greater. One should read the Scriptures with an awareness of this.

*Lenten meeting with the clergy of Rome*
*February 22, 2007*

## 82. *Rereading*

The whole Book is a process of constantly new interpretations where one enters ever more deeply into the mystery proposed at the beginning, and that what was initially present but still closed, unfolds increasingly. In one Book, we can understand the whole journey of Sacred Scripture, which is an ongoing reinterpretation, or rather, a new and better understanding of all that had been said previously.

*Lenten meeting with the clergy of Rome*
*February 22, 2007*

## 83. Scriptura crescet cum legente *[Scripture develops through reading]* (St. Gregory the Great)

An ancient text is reread in another book, let us say 100 years later, and what had been impossible to perceive in that earlier moment, although it was already contained in the previous text, is understood in-depth. And it is read again, ages later, and once again other aspects, other dimensions of the Word are grasped. So it was that Sacred Scripture developed, in this permanent rereading and rewriting in the context of profound continuity, in a continuous succession of the times of waiting. At last, with the coming of Christ and the experience of the Apostles, the Word became definitive. Thus, there can be no further rewriting, but a further deepening of our understanding continues to be necessary. The Lord said: "The Holy Spirit will guide you into depths that you cannot fathom now."

*Encounter with youth in Rome*
*April 6, 2006*

## 84. *Interpreting the Word of God in the Church*

In the Church, Sacred Scripture, the understanding of which increases under the inspiration of the Holy Spirit, and the ministry of its authentic interpretation that was conferred upon the Apostles, are indissolubly bound. Whenever Sacred Scripture is separated from the living voice of the Church, it falls prey to disputes among experts. Of course, all they have to tell us is important and invaluable; the work of scholars is a considerable help in understanding the living process in which the Scriptures developed, hence, also in grasping their historical richness. Yet science alone cannot provide us with a definitive and binding interpretation; it is unable to offer us, in its interpretation, that certainty with which we can live and for which we can even die. A greater mandate is necessary for this, which cannot derive from human abilities alone. The voice of the living Church is essential for this, of the Church entrusted until the end of time to Peter and to the College of the Apostles.

> *Homily at Mass of Possession of the*
> *Chair of the Bishop of Rome*
> *May 7, 2005*

## 85. *In harmony with the Magisterium of the Church*

A fundamental criterion of the method for interpreting the Scriptures [is] harmony with the Church's Magisterium. We should never read Scripture alone because we meet too many closed doors and could easily slip into error. The Bible has been written by the People of God and for the People of God under the inspiration of the Holy Spirit. Only in this communion with the People of God do we truly enter into the "we," into the nucleus of the truth that God himself wants to tell us. . . . An authentic interpretation of the Bible must always be in harmonious accord with the faith of the Catholic Church. It does not treat of an exegesis imposed on this Book from without; the Book is really the voice of the pilgrim People of God and only in the faith of this People are we "correctly attuned" to understand Sacred Scripture.

*General Audience*
*November 14, 2007*

# 2. The Limitations of the Historical-Critical Method of Interpretation

86. *Interpretation of the Bible*

An exegete, an interpreter of Sacred Scripture, must explain it as a historical work "*secundum artem*," that is, with the scientific rigor that we know in accordance with all the historical elements that require it and with the necessary methodology. This alone, however, does not suffice for him to be a theologian. If he were to limit himself to doing this, then theology, or at any rate the interpretation of the Bible, would be something similar to Egyptology or Assyriology, or any other specialization. . . . In this regard, even in the scientific context, theology is always also requested and called into question over and above the scientific perspective. . . . Humanity [is] in need of questions. Whenever questions are no longer asked, even those that concern the essential and go beyond any specialization, we no longer receive answers, either.

*Address to members of the theological faculty*
*of the University of Tübingen, Germany*
*March 21, 2007*

## 87. *Historical-critical exegesis*

Historical-critical exegesis has much to tell us about the past, about the moment when the Word was born, about the meaning it had at the time of Jesus' Apostles; but it does not always give us enough help in understanding that the words of Jesus, of the Apostles and also of the Old Testament, are spirit and life: the Lord of the Old Testament also speaks today.

*Meeting with priests of the Diocese of Albano*
*August 31, 2006*

## 88. *The oneness of Scripture*

The oneness of Scripture is not a purely historical and critical factor but indeed in its entirety, also from the historical viewpoint, it is an inner process of the Word which, read and understood in an ever new way in the course of subsequent *relectures*, continues to develop. This oneness itself, however, is ultimately a theological fact: these writings form one Scripture which can only be properly understood if they are read in the *analogia fidei* as a oneness in which there is progress towards Christ, and inversely, in which Christ draws all history to himself; and if, moreover, all this is brought to life in the Church's faith.

*Address to the bishops of Switzerland*
*November 7, 2006*

## 89. *The question of translation*

It is interesting to point out the criteria which the great biblicist (St. Jerome) abided by in his work as a translator. He himself reveals them when he says that he respects even the order of the words of the Sacred Scriptures, for in them, he says, "the order of the words is also a mystery" (*Epistulae* 57, 5), that is, a revelation.

*General Audience*
*November 7, 2007*

## 90. *The spiritual reading of Sacred Scripture*

I would very much like to see theologians learn to interpret and love Scripture as the Council desired, in accordance with *Dei Verbum*: may they experience the inner unity of Scripture—something that today is helped by "canonical exegesis" (still to be found, of course, in its timid first stages)—and then make a spiritual interpretation of it that is not externally edifying but rather an inner immersion in the presence of the Word. It seems to me a very important task to do something in this regard, to contribute to providing an introduction to living Scripture as an up-to-date Word of God beside, with and in historical-critical exegesis.

*Address to the bishops of Switzerland*
*November 7, 2006*

## 91. *The eternal Word*

Human opinions come and go. What is very modern today will be very antiquated tomorrow. On the other hand, the Word of God is the Word of eternal life, it bears within it eternity and is valid for ever. By carrying the Word of God within us, we therefore carry within us eternity, eternal life.

*General Audience*
*November 7, 2007*

## 92. *The transcendence of Sacred Scripture*

The words of Sacred Scripture always transcend the period in history.

*Homily at Mass on the Feast of the Assumption*
*August 15, 2007*

# VIII. The Word of God in the Life of the Believer

*Ignorance of Scripture is ignorance of Jesus Christ.*

—St. Jerome

93. *Word and time*

God's Word ushers in a new year, it ushers in a period of history. The Word of God is always a renewing force which gives meaning and order to our time.

*Homily at Our Lady Star of Evangelization Parish, Rome*
*December 10, 2006*

# 1. Reading the Bible

94. *Speaking with God*

To read Scripture is to converse with God: "If you pray," [St. Jerome] writes to a young Roman noblewoman, "you speak with the Spouse; if you read, it is he who speaks to you" (*Epistulae* 22, 25).

*General Audience*
*November 14, 2007*

95. *Listening to God*

One must not read Sacred Scripture as one reads any kind of historical book, such as, for example, Homer, Ovid or Horace; it is necessary truly to read it as the Word of God, that is, entering into a conversation with God. One must start by praying and talking to the Lord: "Open the door to me." And what St. Augustine often says in his homilies: "I knocked at the door of the Word to find out at last what the Lord wants to say to me," seems to me to be a very important point. One should not read Scripture in an academic way, but with prayer, saying to the Lord: "Help me to understand your Word, what it is that you want to tell me in this passage."

*Encounter with youth in Rome*
*April 6, 2006*

## 96. Intellectual humility

Intellectual humility is the primary rule for one who searches to penetrate the supernatural realities beginning from the sacred Book. Obviously, humility does not exclude serious study; but to ensure that the results are spiritually beneficial, facilitating true entry into the depth of the text, humility remains indispensable. Only with this interior attitude can one really listen to and eventually perceive the voice of God.

*General Audience*
*June 4, 2008*

## 97. Jerome's instructions

Certainly, to penetrate the Word of God ever more profoundly, a constant and progressive application is needed. Hence, Jerome recommends to the priest Nepotian: "Read the divine Scriptures frequently; rather, may your hands never set the Holy Book down. Learn here what you must teach" (*Epistulae* 52, 7). To the Roman matron Leta he gave this counsel for the Christian education of her daughter: "Ensure that each day she studies some Scripture passage. . . . After prayer, reading should follow, and after reading, prayer. . . . Instead of jewels and silk clothing, may she love the divine Books" (*Epistulae* 107, 9, 12). Through meditation on and knowledge of the Scriptures, one "maintains the equilibrium of the soul" (*Ad Ephesios,* Prologue). Only a profound spirit of prayer and the Holy Spirit's help can introduce us to understanding the Bible: "In the interpretation of Sacred Scripture we always need the help of the Holy Spirit" (*In Michaeam* 1, 1, 10, 15).

*General Audience*
*November 14, 2007*

## 98. *Reading the Bible as a whole*

The Bible as a whole is of course enormous; it must be discovered little by little, for if we take the individual parts on their own, it is often hard to understand that this is the Word of God: I am thinking of certain sections of the Book of Kings with the Chronicles, with the extermination of the peoples who lived in the Holy Land. . . . Therefore, it is only if we take all things as a journey, step by step, and learn to interpret Scripture in its unity, that we can truly have access to the beauty and richness of Sacred Scripture. Consequently, one should read everything, but always mindful of the totality of Sacred Scripture, where one part explains the other, one passage on the journey explains the other.

*Lenten meeting with the clergy of Rome*
*February 22, 2007*

## 99. *Christian reading of the Bible*

The important point is not to fragment Sacred Scripture. The modern critic himself, as we now see, has enabled us to understand that it is an ongoing journey. And we can also see that it is a journey with a direction and that Christ really is its destination. By starting from Christ, we start the entire journey again and enter into the depths of the Word. . . . Sacred Scripture must always be read in the light of Christ.

*Lenten meeting with the clergy of Rome*
*February 22, 2007*

# 2. Reading in the Communion of the Church

### 100. *A communal reading*

This conversation with the Lord in Scripture must always be a conversation that is not only individual but communal, in the great communion of the Church where Christ is ever present, in the communion of the liturgy.

*Meeting with young people in Genoa*
*May 18, 2008*

### 101. *A bidimensional reading*

We must not read Sacred Scripture as a word of the past but as the Word of God that is also addressed to us, and we must try to understand what it is that the Lord wants to tell us. However, to avoid falling into individualism, we must bear in mind that the Word of God has been given to us precisely in order to build communion and to join forces in the truth on our journey towards God. Thus, although it is always a personal Word, it is also a Word that builds community, that builds the Church. We must therefore read it in communion with the living Church.

*General Audience*
*November 7, 2007*

## 102. *In communion*

It is . . . important to read Sacred Scripture and experience Sacred Scripture in the communion of the Church, that is, with all the great witnesses of this Word, beginning with the first Fathers and ending with today's Saints, with today's Magisterium.

*Visit to the Roman Major Seminary*
*February 17, 2007*

## 103. *Growing with Scripture*

In daily contact with Scripture and the Church's teachings, you mature and develop the human, professional and spiritual dimensions, and you can thus enter ever more deeply into the mystery of that creative Reason which continues to love the world and to speak with the freedom of creatures.

*Meeting with members of Sacra Famiglia di Nazareth*
*and Comunità Domenico Tardini associations*
*November 11, 2006*

## 104. *How to read*

I think that we should learn to do three things: to read [Sacred Scripture] in a personal colloquium with the Lord; to read it with the guidance of teachers who have the experience of faith, who have penetrated Sacred Scripture; and to read it in the great company of the Church, in whose liturgy these events never cease to become present anew and in which the Lord speaks with us today. Thus, we may gradually penetrate ever more deeply into Sacred Scripture, in which God truly speaks to us today.

*Encounter with youth in Rome*
*April 6, 2006*

## 105. *Young people and the Word*

The Apostles received the word of salvation and passed it on to their successors as a precious gem kept safely in the jewel box of the Church: without the Church, this pearl runs the risk of being lost or destroyed. My dear young friends, love the word of God and love the Church, and this will give you access to a treasure of very great value and will teach you how to appreciate its richness.

*Message for the Twenty-First World Youth Day*
*February 22, 2006*

# 3. Reading Advice

### 106. *Current relevance of the Sacred Scriptures*

Sometimes, when I was still a teacher in my Country, young people had read the Sacred Scriptures. And they read them as one reads the text of a poem one has not understood. Naturally, to learn to say words correctly one must first understand the text with its drama, with its immediacy.

*Meeting with the priests of the Diocese of Albano*
*August 31, 2006*

### 107. *Reading during free time*

Having more free time, one can dedicate oneself more easily to conversation with God, meditation on Sacred Scripture and reading [of] some useful, formative book. Those who experience this spiritual repose know how useful it is not to reduce vacations to mere relaxation and amusement.

*Angelus*
*August 13, 2006*

108. *The Bible in the family*

The Christian family passes on the faith when parents teach their children to pray and when they pray with them [cf. *Familiaris Consortio*, no. 60]; when they lead them to the sacraments and gradually introduce them to the life of the Church; when all join in reading the Bible, letting the light of faith shine on their family life and praising God as our Father.

*Homily at Mass for the Fifth World Meeting of Families*
*July 9, 2006*

109. *A personal memory*

Already as a boy, helped by my parents and by the parish priest, I had discovered the beauty of the Liturgy, and I came to love it more and more because I felt that divine beauty appears in it and that Heaven unfolds before us. The second element was the discovery of the beauty of knowledge, of knowing God and Sacred Scripture, thanks to which it is possible to enter into that great adventure of dialogue with God which is theology.

*Encounter with youth in Rome*
*April 6, 2006*

## 110. *The seminary years*

I can say that Sacred Scripture really was the soul of our theological studies [during my time in seminary]: we truly lived with Sacred Scripture and learned to love it, to converse with it.

*Visit to the Roman Major Seminary*
*February 17, 2007*

## 111. *To young people*

My dear young friends, I urge you to become familiar with the Bible, and to have it at hand so that it can be your compass pointing out the road to follow. By reading it, you will learn to know Christ.

*Message for the Twenty-First World Youth Day*
*February 22, 2006*

# 4. Reading and Life

### 112. *Sacred Scripture and humanism*

We see precisely today how the education of the personality in its totality, the education to responsibility before God and man, is the true condition of all progress, all peace, all reconciliation and the exclusion of violence. Education before God and man: it is Sacred Scripture that offers us the guide for education and thus of true humanism.

*General Audience*
*November 14, 2007*

### 113. *Word and witness*

Word and witness go together: the Word calls forth and gives form to the witness; the witness derives its authenticity from total fidelity to the Word, as expressed and lived in the apostolic community of faith under the guidance of the Holy Spirit.

*Address to representatives of the*
*Lutheran World Federation*
*November 7, 2005*

## 114. *The Gospel and society*

Social issues and the Gospel are inseparable. When we bring people only knowledge, ability, technical competence and tools, we bring them too little. All too quickly the mechanisms of violence take over: the capacity to destroy and to kill becomes dominant, becomes the way to gain power—a power which at some point should bring law, but which will never be able to do so.

*Homily at Mass in Munich*
*September 10, 2006*


## 115. *A Word that builds*

May the reading of the Word of God, the renewal of the revelation of Sinai after the Exile, serve then for communion with God and among men and women. This communion is expressed in the rebuilding of the temple, the city and its walls. The Word of God and the rebuilding of the city in the Book of Nehemiah are closely connected: on the one hand, without the Word of God there is neither city nor community; on the other, the Word of God does not remain only a discourse but leads to constructing, it is a Word that builds.

*Homily at Our Lady Star of Evangelization Parish, Rome*
*December 10, 2006*

116. *The Word of God and progress*

Where the Word of God does not exist, development fails to function and has no positive results. Only if God's Word is put first, only if man is reconciled with God, can material things also go smoothly.

*Homily at Mass in St. Anne's Parish, Vatican City*
*February 5, 2006*

117. *The Word and images*

Wherever there is true and profound meditation on the Word, wherever we truly enter into contemplation of this visibility, this tangibility of God in the world, new images are also born, new possibilities of making the events of salvation visible.

*Meeting with priests and clergy of the Diocese of Rome*
*February 7, 2008*

## 118. *The Gospel of love*

The Gospel does not humiliate human freedom and authentic social progress; on the contrary, it helps human beings to fulfill themselves completely and renews society through the gentle and exacting law of love.

> *Address to the bishops of Lithuania, Latvia,*
> *and Estonia on their* ad limina *visit*
> *June 23, 2006*

## 119. *Hope and the Word*

Christian hope, rooted in a solid faith in the Word of Christ, is the anchor of salvation that helps us overcome seemingly insurmountable difficulties and allows us to glimpse the light of joy beyond the darkness of pain and death.

> *Homily at Mass in the Vatican*
> *October 16, 2006*

# IX. THE
# *LECTIO DIVINA*

*Attend assiduously to prayer and the* lectio divina.
*When you pray, you speak with God; when you
read [Scripture], it is God who speaks with you.*

—ST. CYPRIAN OF CARTHAGE

120. *The method of the* lectio

Sacred Scripture introduces one into communion with the
family of God. Thus, one should not read Sacred Scripture
on one's own. Of course, it is always important to read the
Bible in a very personal way, in a personal conversation
with God; but at the same time, it is important to read it in
the company of people with whom one can advance, letting
oneself be helped by the great masters of *lectio divina*.

*Encounter with youth in Rome
April 6, 2006*

### 121. *Efficaciousness of the* lectio

I would like in particular to recall and recommend the ancient tradition of *Lectio divina*: the diligent reading of Sacred Scripture accompanied by prayer brings about that intimate dialogue in which the person reading hears God who is speaking, and in praying, responds to him with trusting openness of heart (cf. *Dei Verbum*, no. 25).

*Address on the fortieth anniversary of* Dei Verbum
*September 16, 2005*

### 122. *Rumination*

[*Lectio divina*] consists in pouring over a biblical text for some time, reading it and rereading it, as it were, "ruminating" on it as the Fathers say and squeezing from it, so to speak, all its "juice," so that it may nourish meditation and contemplation and, like water, succeed in irrigating life itself. One condition for *lectio divina* is that the mind and heart be illumined by the Holy Spirit, that is, by the same Spirit who inspired the Scriptures, and that they be approached with an attitude of "reverential hearing."

*Angelus*
*November 6, 2005*

## 123. *Origen's recommendations*

In his *Letter to Gregory*, Origen recommends: "Study first of all the *lectio* of the divine Scriptures. Study them, I say. For we need to study the divine writings deeply . . . and while you study these divine works with a believing and God-pleasing intention, knock at that which is closed in them and it shall be opened to you by the porter, of whom Jesus says, 'To him the gatekeeper opens.' While you attend to this *lectio divina*, seek aright and with unwavering faith in God the hidden sense which is present in most passages of the divine Scriptures. And do not be content with knocking and seeking, for what is absolutely necessary for understanding divine things is *oratio*, and in urging us to this the Savior says not only 'knock and it will be opened to you,' and 'seek and you will find,' but also 'ask and it will be given you'" (*Epistula ad Gregorium*, 4). The "*primordial role*" played by Origen in the history of *lectio divina* instantly flashes before one's eyes. Bishop Ambrose of Milan, who learned from Origen's works to interpret the Scriptures, later introduced them into the West to hand them on to Augustine and to the monastic tradition that followed.

*General Audience*
*May 2, 2007*

## 124. *Ambrose and* lectio divina

Culturally well-educated but at the same time ignorant of the Scriptures, [St. Ambrose] briskly began to study them. From the works of Origen, the indisputable master of the "Alexandrian School," he learned to know and to comment on the Bible. Thus, Ambrose transferred to the Latin environment the meditation on the Scriptures which Origen had begun, introducing in the West the practice of *lectio divina*. The method of *lectio* served to guide all of Ambrose's preaching and writings, which stemmed precisely from *prayerful listening* to the Word of God.

*General Audience*
*October 24, 2007*

## 125. *Augustine's "hearing in the heart"*

Augustine learned from the life and example of Bishop Ambrose to believe and to preach. We can refer to a famous sermon of the African, which centuries later merited citation in the conciliar Constitution on Divine Revelation, *Dei Verbum*: "Therefore, all clerics, particularly priests of Christ and others who, as deacons or catechists, [who] are officially engaged in the ministry of the Word," *Dei Verbum* recommends, "should immerse themselves in the Scriptures by constant sacred reading and diligent study. For it must not happen that anyone becomes"—and this is [the citation of Augustine]—"'an empty preacher of the Word of God to others, not being a hearer of the Word in his own heart'" (*Dei Verbum*, no. 25). Augustine had learned precisely from Ambrose how to "hear in his own heart" this perseverance in reading Sacred Scripture with a prayerful approach, so as truly to absorb and assimilate the Word of God in one's heart.

General Audience
October 24, 2007

126. *The structure of* lectio divina

A time-honored way to study and savor the word of God is *lectio divina* which constitutes a real and veritable *spiritual journey* marked out in stages. After the *lectio*, which consists of reading and rereading a passage from Sacred Scripture and taking in the main elements, we proceed to *meditatio*. This is a moment of interior reflection in which the soul turns to God and tries to understand what his word is saying to us today. Then comes *oratio* in which we linger to talk with God directly. Finally we come to *contemplatio*. This helps us to keep our hearts attentive to the presence of Christ whose word is "a lamp shining in a dark place, until the day dawns and the morning star rises in your hearts" (2 Pt 1:19). Reading, study and meditation of the Word should then flow into a life of consistent fidelity to Christ and his teachings.

Message for the Twenty-First World Youth Day
February 22, 2006

127. Lectio et oratio *[reading and praying]*

We should know Jesus in an increasingly personal way, listening to him, living together with him, staying with him. Listening to him—in *lectio divina*, that is, reading Sacred Scripture in a non-academic but spiritual way; thus, we learn to encounter Jesus present, who speaks to us. We must reason and reflect, before him and with him, on his words and actions. The reading of Sacred Scripture is prayer, it must be prayer—it must emerge from prayer and lead to prayer.

*Homily at Holy Thursday Chrism Mass*
*April 13, 2006*

128. *Thinking with Christ*

The Apostle [Paul invites us to] think with Christ's thoughts [cf. Phil 2:5]. And we can do so by reading Sacred Scripture in which Christ's thoughts are the Word, they speak to us. In this sense we must practice *lectio divina*, we must grasp Christ's way of thinking in the Scriptures, we must learn to think with Christ, to think Christ's thoughts and thus feel Christ's sentiments, to be able to convey Christ's thinking to others.

*Reflection during the Liturgy of the Hours*
*October 3, 2005*

## 129. *Schools of prayer*

We must increase the number of . . . schools of prayer, for praying together, where it is possible to learn personal prayer in all its dimensions: as silent listening to God, as a listening that penetrates his Word, penetrates his silence, sounds the depths of his action in history and in one's own person; and to understand his language in one's life and then to learn to respond in prayer with the great prayers of the Psalms of the Old Testament and prayers of the New.

> *Address to the bishops of Switzerland*
> *November 9, 2006*

## 130. *Beyond the* lectio

To build your life on Christ, to accept the word with joy and put its teachings into practice: this, young people of the third millennium, should be your program! There is an urgent need for the emergence of a new generation of apostles anchored firmly in the word of Christ, capable of responding to the challenges of our times and prepared to spread the Gospel far and wide.

> *Message for the Twenty-First World Youth Day*
> *February 22, 2006*

# INDEX

*(Numbering refers to the sequential positioning of each thought.)*

*Mary:*
"Dwelling Place" of the Word, 28-29
hearing the Word, 27
*Pastoral initiative:*
in favor of Sacred Scripture, 66
*Prayer:*
and reading, 94, 127, 129
and the Word of God, 59
*Priest:*
and Sacred Scripture, 62
*Proclamation:*
of the Word of God, 56-59
*Progress:* 116
*Reading:*
of the Bible in families, 108
communal, of the Scriptures, 100-102
community of the Scriptures, 42, 74
and re-reading of Sacred Scripture, 82, 88
of Sacred Scripture, 97-99, 103-104, 106-107, 110
spiritual, of the Scriptures, 55, 90
*Religious, men and women:*
and Sacred Scripture, 63
*Scripture, Sacred:*
ecclesiality of, 36
oneness of, 88
voice of God, 19
*Theology:*
and exegesis, 80, 86
*Tradition:*
and Sacred Scripture, 45

# Related Titles

## St. Paul
*Spiritual Thoughts Series*
Unite yourselves with Christ! Let Pope Benedict XVI teach you how to share the gift of Christ with the world like St. Paul did. Every page has a thought from the Pope about St. Paul's life and writings. Use the space in the book to record your own thoughts. Read, grow your biblical literacy, and dive into St. Paul's writings. A book for everyone seeking Christ.
English: No. 7-053, 128 pp.

## Mary
*Spiritual Thoughts Series*
Embrace Mary, the Mother of God and all Christians! Pope Benedict XVI shares his thoughts on Mary as the Mother of God in this book. Let the Holy Father's explanation of the special Catholic understanding of Mary's mystery enrich your faith journey. For all Christians who want to learn more about Mary.
English: No. 7-054, 172 pp.

## The Saints
*Spiritual Thoughts Series*
Be inspired by Pope Benedict XVI's thoughts about ancient and modern saints. The Holy Father shows how the saints glorified God despite difficulties. Find faith, cling to hope, and learn to love as you read these selections on the saints from the Pope's writings, speeches, and sermons. A book for all Christians.
English: No. 7-055, 164 pp.

To order these resources or to obtain a catalog of other USCCB titles, visit *www.usccbpublishing.org* or call toll-free 800-235-8722. In the Washington metropolitan area or from outside the United States, call 202-722-8716. Para pedidos en español, llame al 800-235-8722 y presione 4 para hablar con un representante del servicio al cliente en español.